SEEDS

OF

INSPIRATIONS

Motivating Quotes for You and Your Students

JILL BODDENBERG

8102 Lemont Road,
#300, Woodridge, IL 60517, U.S.A.
Phone: 630-390-3580   Fax: 630-390-3585

Compiled by Jill Boddenberg

Cover Design by Design Dynamics

Published by Great Quotations, Inc.

Library of Congress Catalog Card Number: 98-075781

ISBN 1-56245-373-4

Printed in Hong Kong 2002

"The future belongs to those who believe in the beauty of their dreams."

— ELEANOR ROOSEVELT

"Accept the challenges, so that you may feel the exhilaration of victory."

— GENERAL GEORGE S. PATTON

"We are
continually
faced by great
opportunities
brilliantly
disguised as
insolvable
problems."

"Do not follow where the path may lead....Go instead where there is no path and leave a trail."

"Well done is better than well said."

— BEN FRANKLIN

"The greatest
thing in this world
is not so much
where we are, but
in what direction
we are moving."

— O.W. HOLMES

"Make the
mistakes of
yesterday your
lessons for
today."

> "The only limit to our realization of tomorrow will be our doubts of today."

— FRANKLIN D. ROOSEVELT

"When nothing seems to help,
I go and look at a stonecutter
hammering away at his rock
perhaps a hundred times
without as much as a crack
showing in it. Yet at the
hundred and first blow it will
spilt in two, and I know it was
not that blow that did it — but
all that had gone before."

— JACOB RIIS

"It is a funny thing about life; if you refuse to accept anything but the best, you very often get it."

— SOMERSET MAUGHAM

"Act as though it were impossible to fail."

"Destiny is not a matter of chance; it is a matter of choice."

"Unless you try to do something beyond what you have already mastered, you will never grow."

— RALPH WALDO EMERSON

"If you've made up your mind you can do something, you're absolutely right."

"The difference between the impossible and the possible lies in a person's determination."

— TOMMY LASORDA
Major League Manager

"We cannot direct the wind . . . but we can adjust the sails."

"Do not let what you cannot do interfere with what you can do."

— JOHN WOODEN
College Basketball Coach

"Failure is not
the worst thing
in the world.
The very worst is
not to try."

"Success is a journey, not a destination."

— BEN SWEETLAND

"Inch by inch,
life's a cinch.

Yard by yard,
life is hard."

"It is never too late to be what you might have become."

— GEORGE ELIOT

"The journey of a thousand miles starts with a single step."

— CHINESE PROVERB

"Good intentions
are no substitute
for action; failure
usually follows
the path of least
persistence."

"People can alter their lives by altering their attitudes."

— WILLIAM JAMES

"The greatest
mistake a person
can make is to
be afraid of
making one."

— ELBERT HUBBARD

"The golden opportunity you are seeking is in yourself. It is not in your environment; it is not in luck or chance, or the help of others; it is in yourself alone."

— ORISON SWETT MARDEN

"Failure
is success
if we learn
from it."

— MALCOLM S. FORBES

"Don't wait for your ship to come in; swim out to it."

"Cherish your visions and your dreams as they are the children of your soul — the blueprints of your ultimate achievements."

— NAPOLEON HILL

"In the middle of difficulty lies opportunity."

— ALBERT EINSTEIN

"People with
goals succeed
because they
know where
they're going."

— EARL NIGHTINGALE

"Keep trying.
It's only from
the valley that
the mountain
seems high."

"The price of success is perseverance. The price of failure comes cheaper."

"Failure is only
the opportunity
to begin
again more
intelligently."

— HENRY FORD

"One cannot change yesterday, but only make the most of today, and look with hope toward tomorrow."

"People rarely succeed at anything unless they have fun doing it."

"Those who bring sunshine to the lives of others cannot keep it from themselves."

— JAMES BARRIE

"Most people are about as happy as they make up their minds to be."

— ABRAHAM LINCOLN

"Happiness is not the absence of conflict, but the ability to cope with it."

"Whether you think you can or think you can't — you are right."

— HENRY FORD

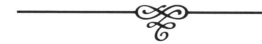

"The mind, like a parachute, functions only when open."

"Happiness lies in the joy of achievement and the thrill of creative effort."

— FRANKLIN ROOSEVELT

"Use the talents
you possess, for
the woods would
be very silent if
no birds sang
except the best."

"*Did* is a word of
achievement;
Won't is a word of retreat;
Might is a word of
bereavement;
Can't is a word of defeat;
Ought is a word of duty;
Try is a word each hour;
Will is a word of beauty;
Can is a word of power."

"It's your attitude and not your aptitude that determines your altitude."

— ZIG ZIGLAR

"You may not have been responsible for your heritage, but you are responsible for your future."

"The difference between ordinary and extraordinary is that little extra."

"When we have done our best, we should wait the result in peace."

— J. LUBBOCK

"It is one of
the most beautiful
compensations of
this life that no man
can sincerely try to
help another without
helping himself."

— RALPH WALDO EMERSON

"If a man is called to be a streetsweeper, he should sweep streets even as Michelangelo painted, or Beethoven composed music, or Shakespeare wrote poetry. He should sweep streets so well that all the hosts of heaven and earth will pause to say, here lived a great streetsweeper who did his job well."

— MARTIN LUTHER KING, JR.

"The quality of a person's life is in direct proportion to their commitment to excellence, regardless of their chosen field of endeavor."

— VINCENT T. LOMBARDI

"Genius is the ability to reduce the complicated to the simple."

— C.W. CERAN

"Far away, there in the sunshine, are my highest aspirations. I may not reach them, but I can look up and see their beauty, believe in them and try to follow where they lead."

— LOUISA MAY ALCOTT

"There's no thrill in easy sailing when the skies are clear and blue; there's no joy in merely doing things which any one can do. But there is some satisfaction that is mighty sweet to take, when you reach a destination that you thought you'd never make."

— SPIRELLA

"Luck is what happens when preparation meets opportunity."

— ELMER LETTERMAN

"The harder you work the luckier you get."

— **GARY PLAYER**
Golfer

"The difference between a successful person and others is not a lack of strength, not a lack of knowledge, but rather in a lack of will."

— VINCENT T. LOMBARDI

"You must begin to think of yourself as becoming the person you want to be."

— DAVID VISCOTT

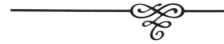

"Live your life each day as you would climb a mountain. An occasional glance toward the summit keeps the goal in mind, but many beautiful scenes are to be observed from each new vantage point. Climb slowly, steadily, enjoying each passing moment, and the view from the summit will serve as a fitting climax for the journey."

— HAROLD V. MELCHERT

"Obstacles are
what you see
when you take
your eyes off
your goals."

"Aerodynamically
the bumble bee
shouldn't be able to
fly, but the bumble
bee doesn't know it
so it goes on flying
anyway."

— MARY KAY ASH

"No one can make you feel inferior without your permission."

"When we give it our all, we can live with ourselves — regardless of the results."

"The best portion
of a good life is the
little nameless,
unremembered
acts of kindness
and of love."

— WILLIAM WORDSWORTH

"Real leaders
are ordinary
people with
extraordinary
determination."

"The courage to speak must be matched by the wisdom to listen."

"Better keep
yourself clean and
bright; you are the
window through
which you must see
the world.

— GEORGE BERNARD SHAW

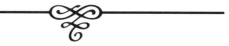

"You will find as you look back upon your life that the moments that stand out, the moments when you have really lived, are the moments when you have done things in a spirit of love."

— HENRY DRUMMOND

"People forget how fast you did a job — but they remember how well you did it."

— HOWARD W. NEWTON

"Regardless of your past, your future is a clean slate."

"Yesterday is a cancelled check; tomorrow is a promissory note; today is the only cash you have — so spend it wisely."

— KAY LYONS

"Every job is
a self-portrait
of the person
who did it."

"Do not wish to be anything but what you are, and try to be that perfectly."

— ST. FRANCIS DE SALES

"Whatever happens, do not lose hold of the two main ropes of life — hope and faith."

"We don't need
more strength
or more ability
or greater
opportunity. What
we need is to use
what we have."

— BASIL S. WALSH

"It takes both rain and sunshine to make a rainbow."

"The highest reward for a person's toil is not what they get for it, but what they become by it."

— JOHN RUSKIN

Other Titles by Great Quotations, Inc.

rd Covers

cient Echoes
hold the Golfer
mmanders in Chief
e Essence of Music
st Ladies
od Lies for Ladies
eat Quotes From Great Teachers
eat Women
hought of You Today
urney to Success
t Between Friends
sting Impressions
Husband My Love
ver Ever Give Up
e Passion of Chocolate
ace Be With You
e Perfect Brew
e Power of Inspiration
aring the Season
ldy Bears
ere's No Place Like Home

Paperbacks

301 Ways to Stay Young
ABC's of Parenting
Angel-grams
African American Wisdom
Astrology for Cats
Astrology for Dogs
The Be-Attitudes
Birthday Astrologer
Can We Talk
Chocoholic Reasonettes
Cornerstones of Success
Daddy & Me
Erasing My Sanity
Graduation is Just the Beginning
Grandma I Love You
Happiness is Found Along the Way
Hooked on Golf
Ignorance is Bliss
In Celebration of Women
Inspirations
Interior Design for Idiots

Great Quotations, Inc.
8102 Lemont Road,
#300, Woodridge, IL 60517, U.S.A.
Phone: 630-390-3580   Fax: 630-390-3585

Other Titles by Great Quotations, Inc.

Paperbacks

I'm Not Over the Hill
Life's Lessons
Looking for Mr. Right
Midwest Wisdom
Mommy & Me
Mother, I Love You
The Mother Load
Motivating Quotes
Mrs.Murphy's Laws
Mrs. Webster's Dictionary
Only A Sister
The Other Species
Parenting 101
Pink Power
Romantic Rhapsody
The Secret Langauge of Men
The Secret Langauge of Women
The Secrets in Your Name
A Servant's Heart
Social Disgraces
Stress or Sanity
A Teacher is Better Than
Teenage of Insanity
Touch of Friendship
Wedding Wonders
Words From the Coach

Perpetual Calendars

365 Reasons to Eat Chocolate
Always Remember Who Loves Yo
Best Friends
Coffee Breaks
The Dog Ate My Car Keys
Extraordinary Women
Foundations of Leadership
Generations
The Heart That Loves
The Honey Jar
I Think My Teacher Sleeps at Scho
I'm a Little Stressed
Keys to Success
Kid Stuff
Never Never Give Up
Older Than Dirt
Secrets of a Successful Mom
Shopoholic
Sweet Dreams
Teacher Zone
Tee Times
A Touch of Kindness
Apple a Day
Golf Forever
Quotes From Great Women
Teacher Are First Class